Lil Miss Melanie's ♡ Melanin

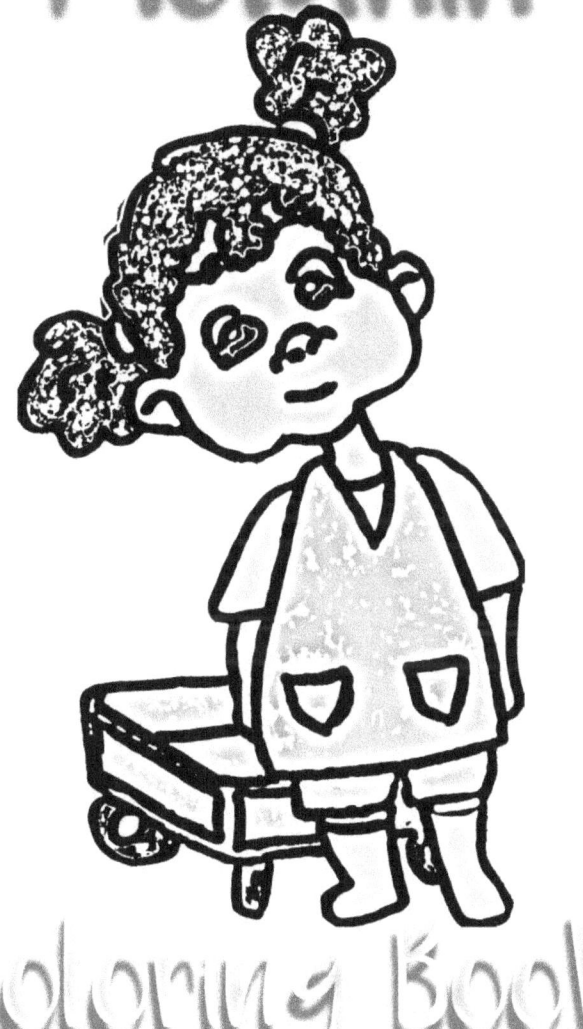

Coloring Book

Designed By Chenae Glaze-Cook

Copyright © 2018 Deiarra Glaze-Cook

All rights reserved.

ISBN: 1986857085
ISBN-13: 978-1986857086

Daily Affirmation 1: I AM BEAUTIFUL..

(Draw a picture of yourself below)

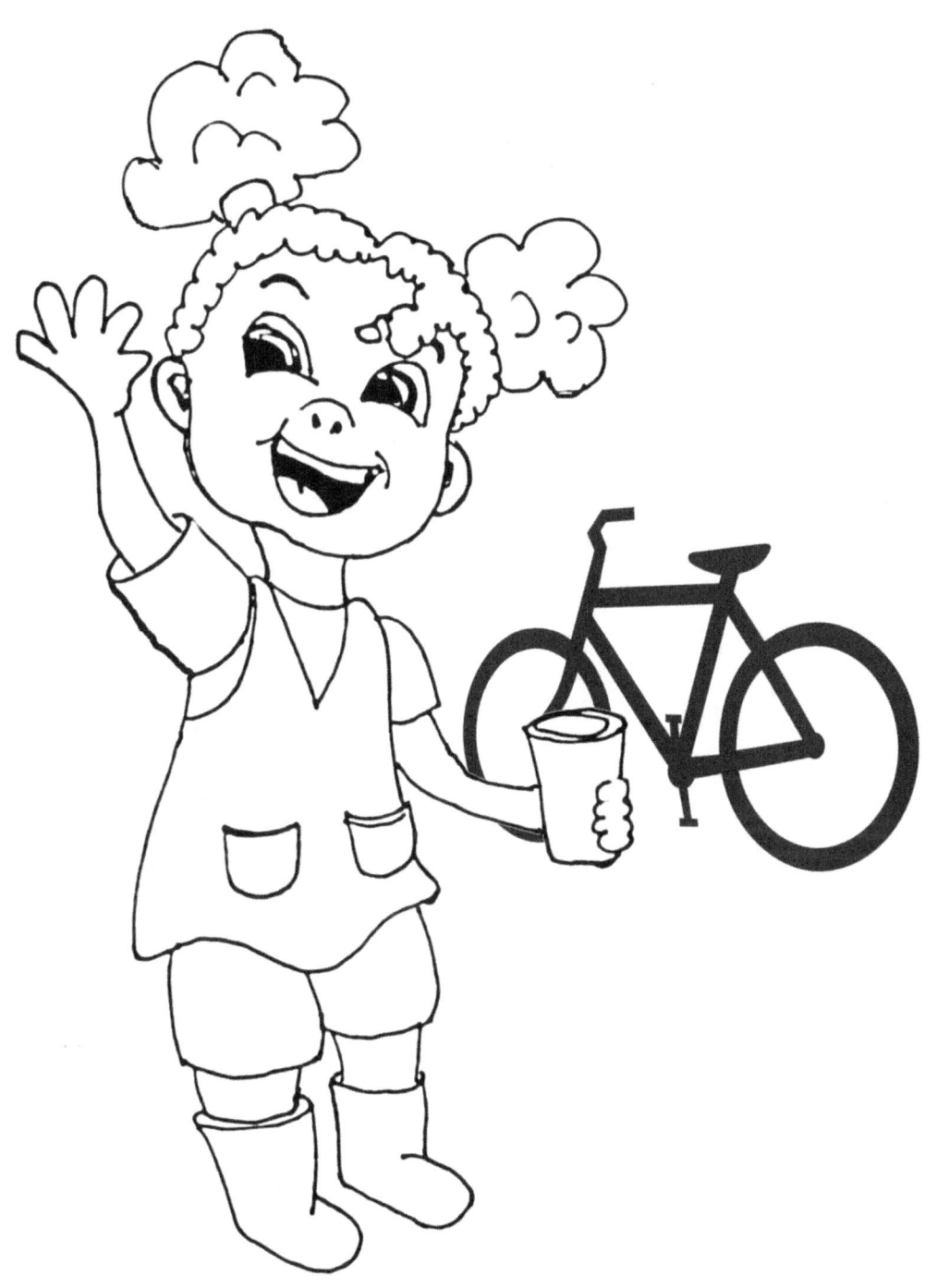

Daily Affirmation 2:
I AM SMART.

(Draw a picture of what you learned today below.)

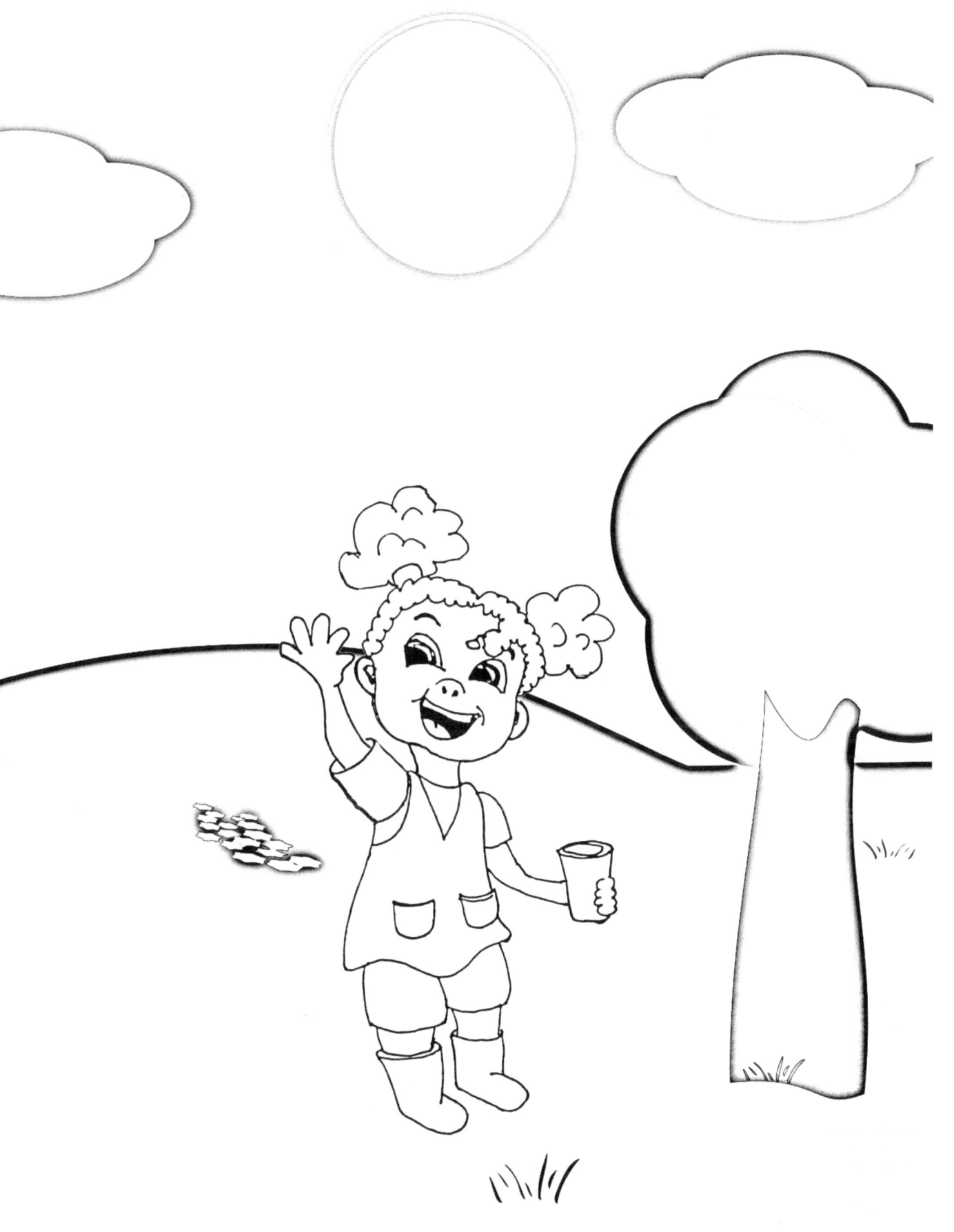

Daily Affirmation 3:
I AM RESPECTFUL.

(Draw a picture of someone you respect below.)

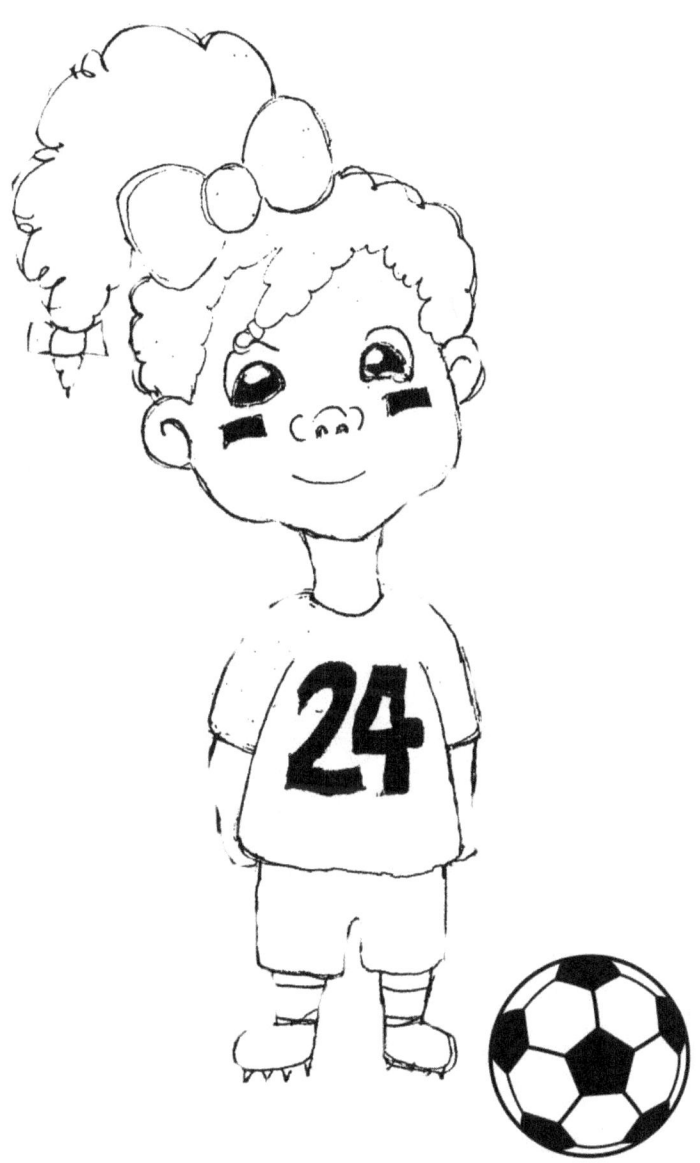

Daily Affirmation 4:
I AM TRUSTWORTHY.

(Draw a picture of you helping someone below.)

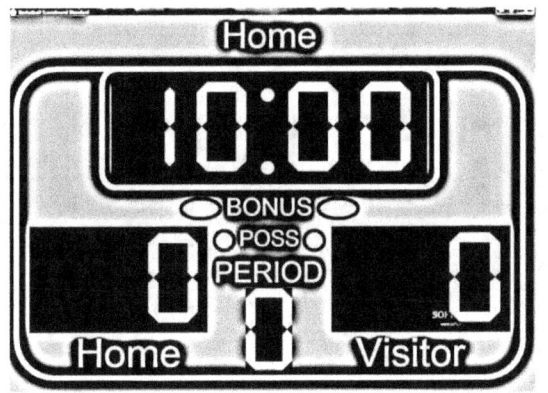

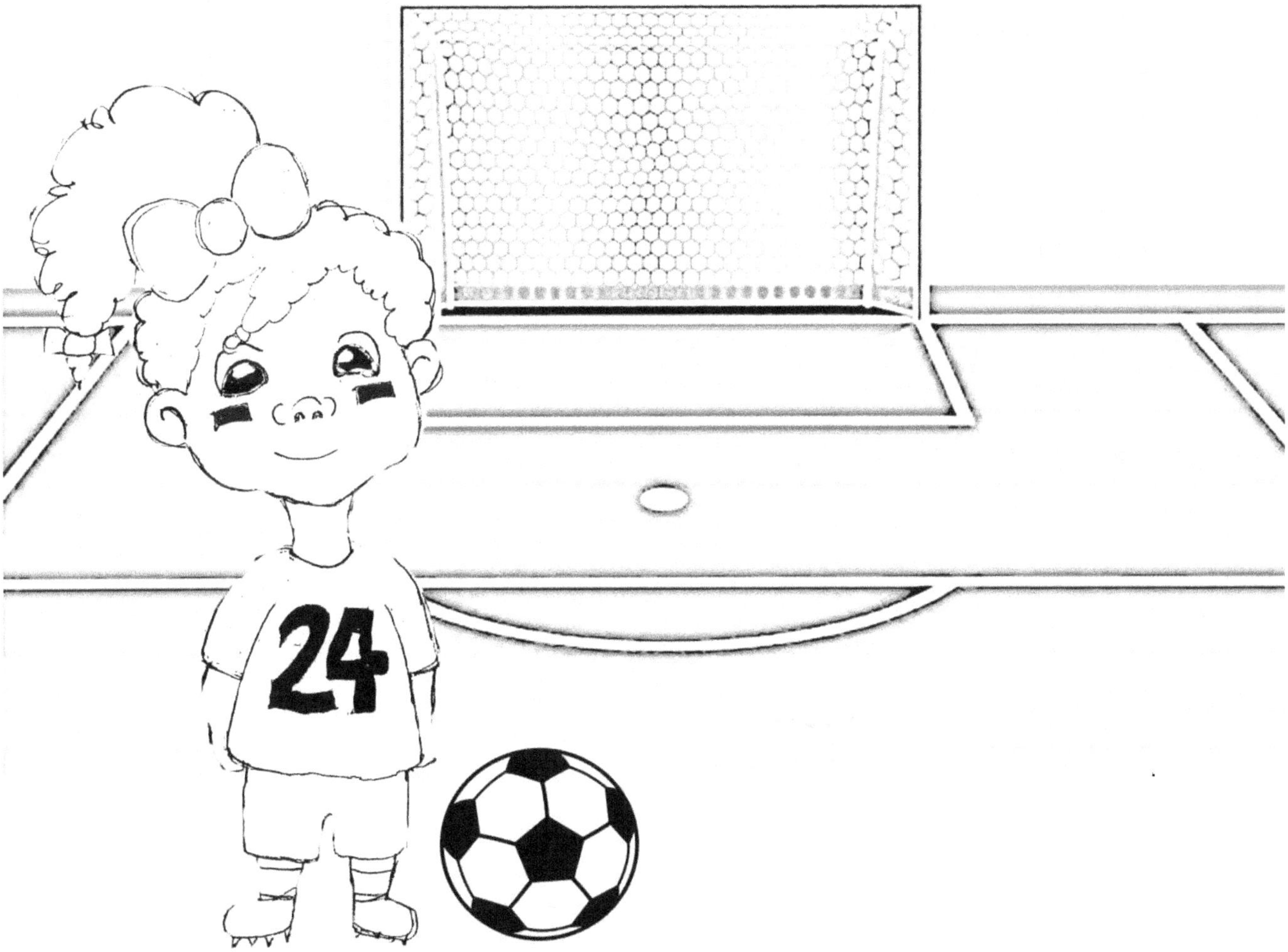

Daily Affirmation 5:
I AM HARD-WORKING.

(Draw a picture of you doing your chores below.)

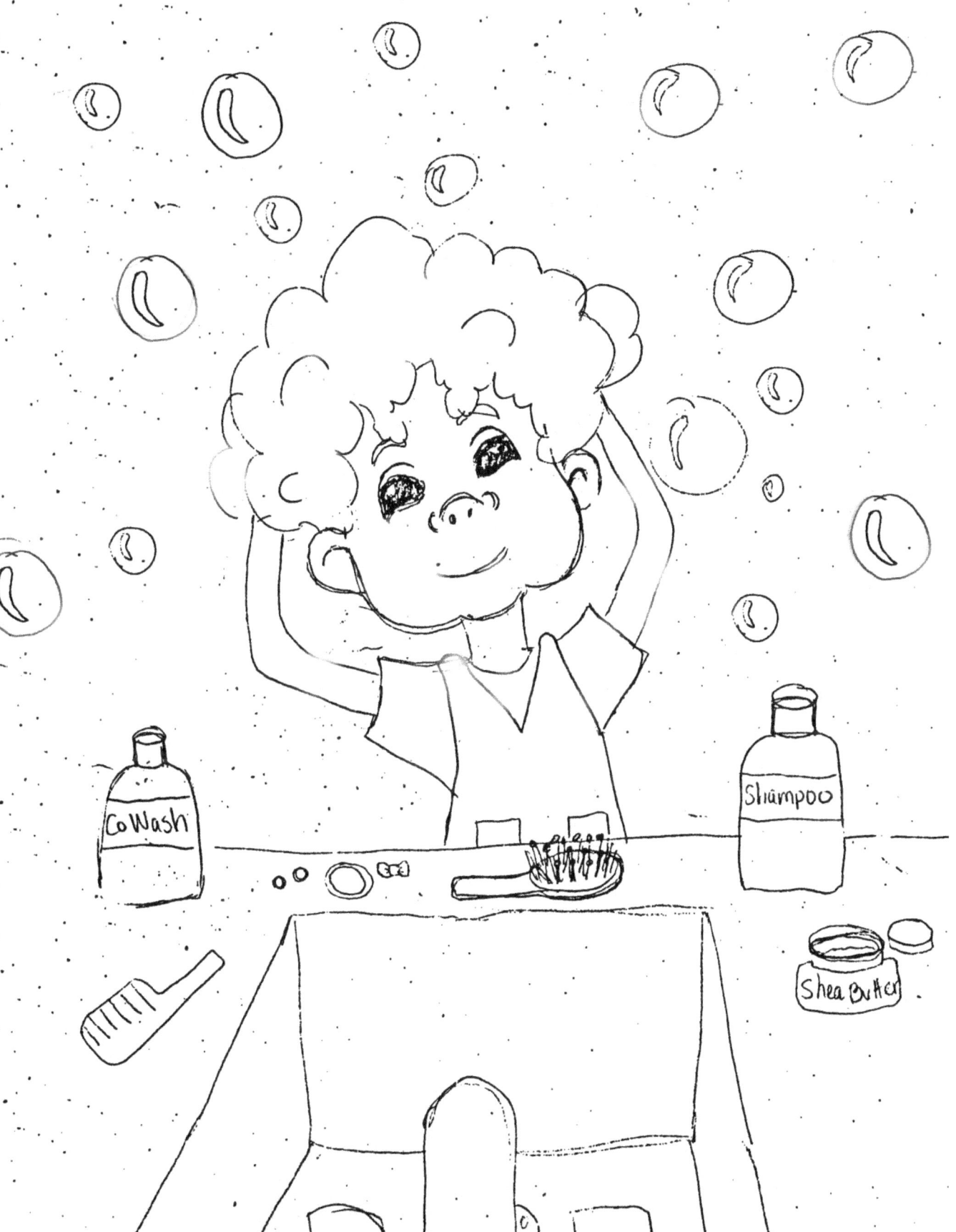

Daily Affirmation 6:
I AM IMPORTANT.

(Draw a picture of what you want to be when you grow up.)

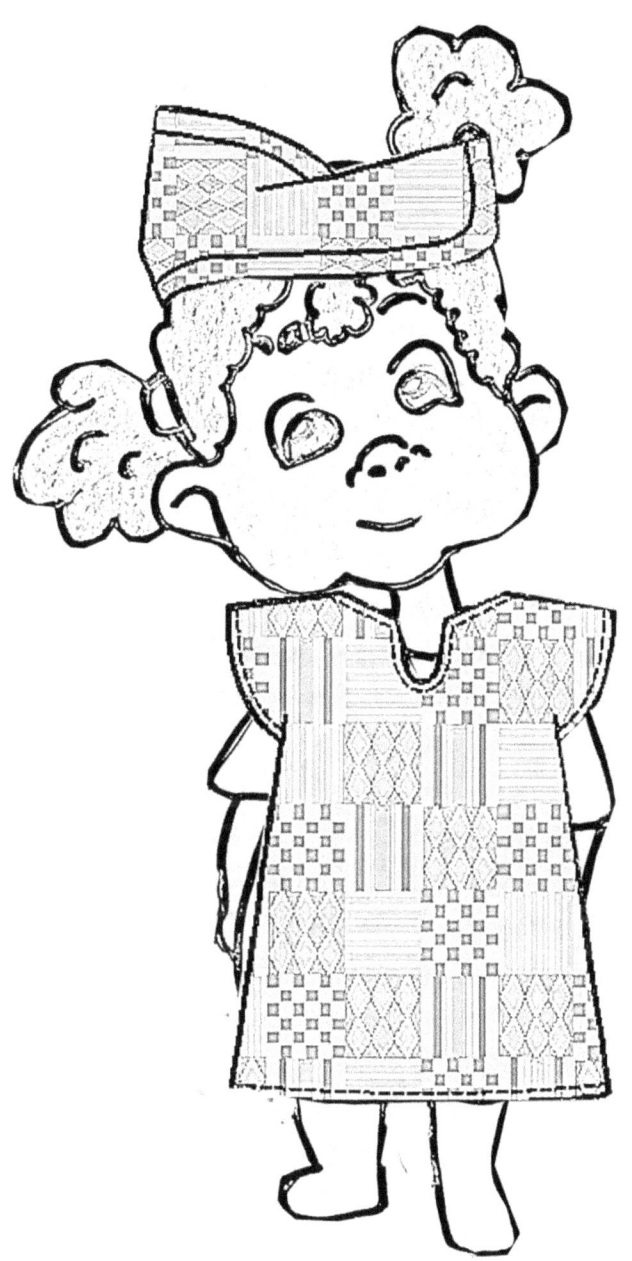

Daily Affirmation #7:
I AM A YOUNG QUEEN.

(Draw a picture of yourself as a QUEEN.)

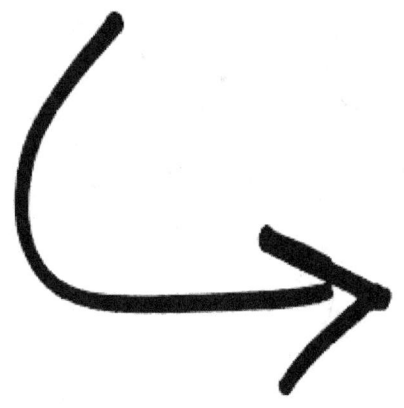

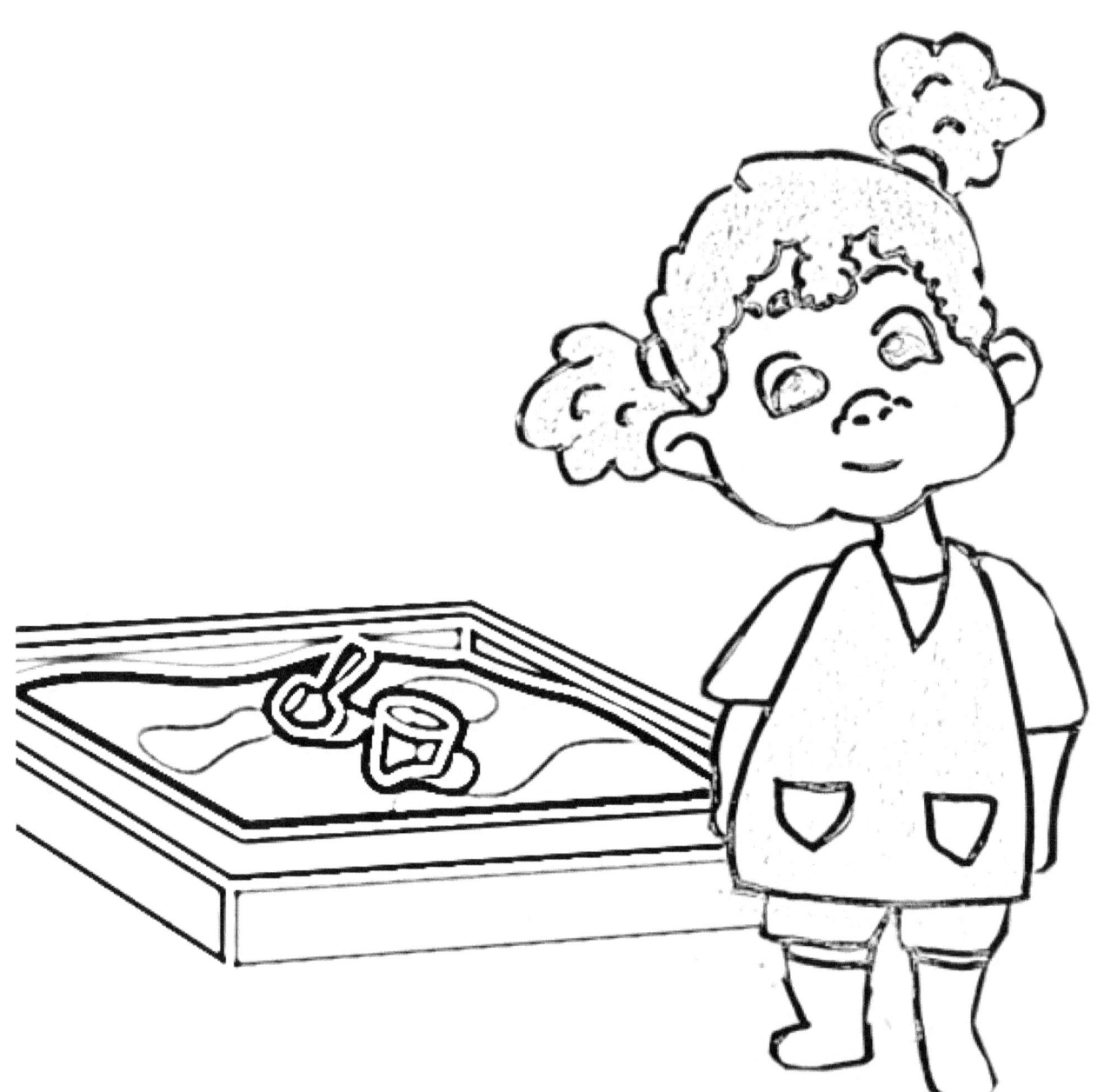

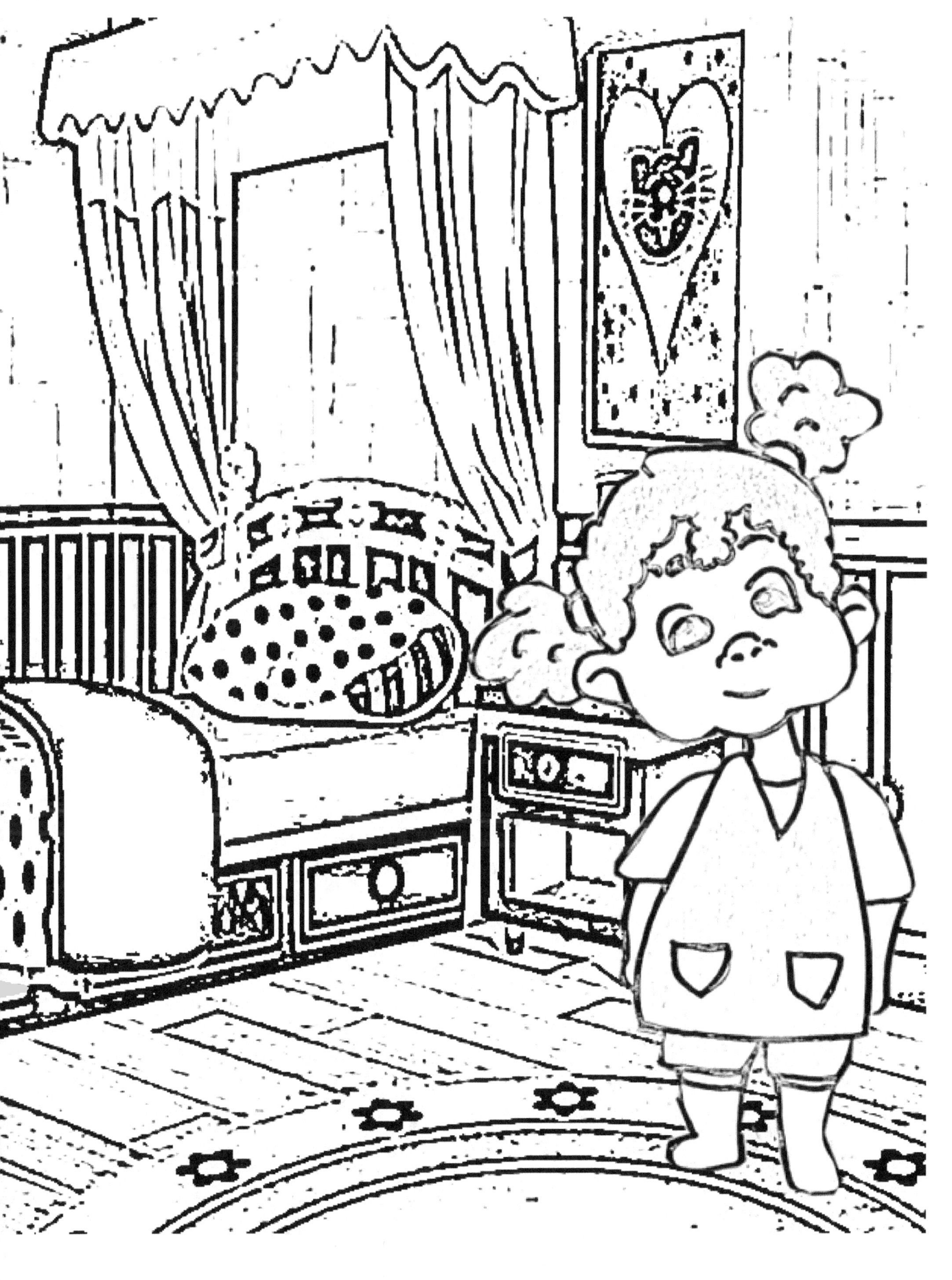

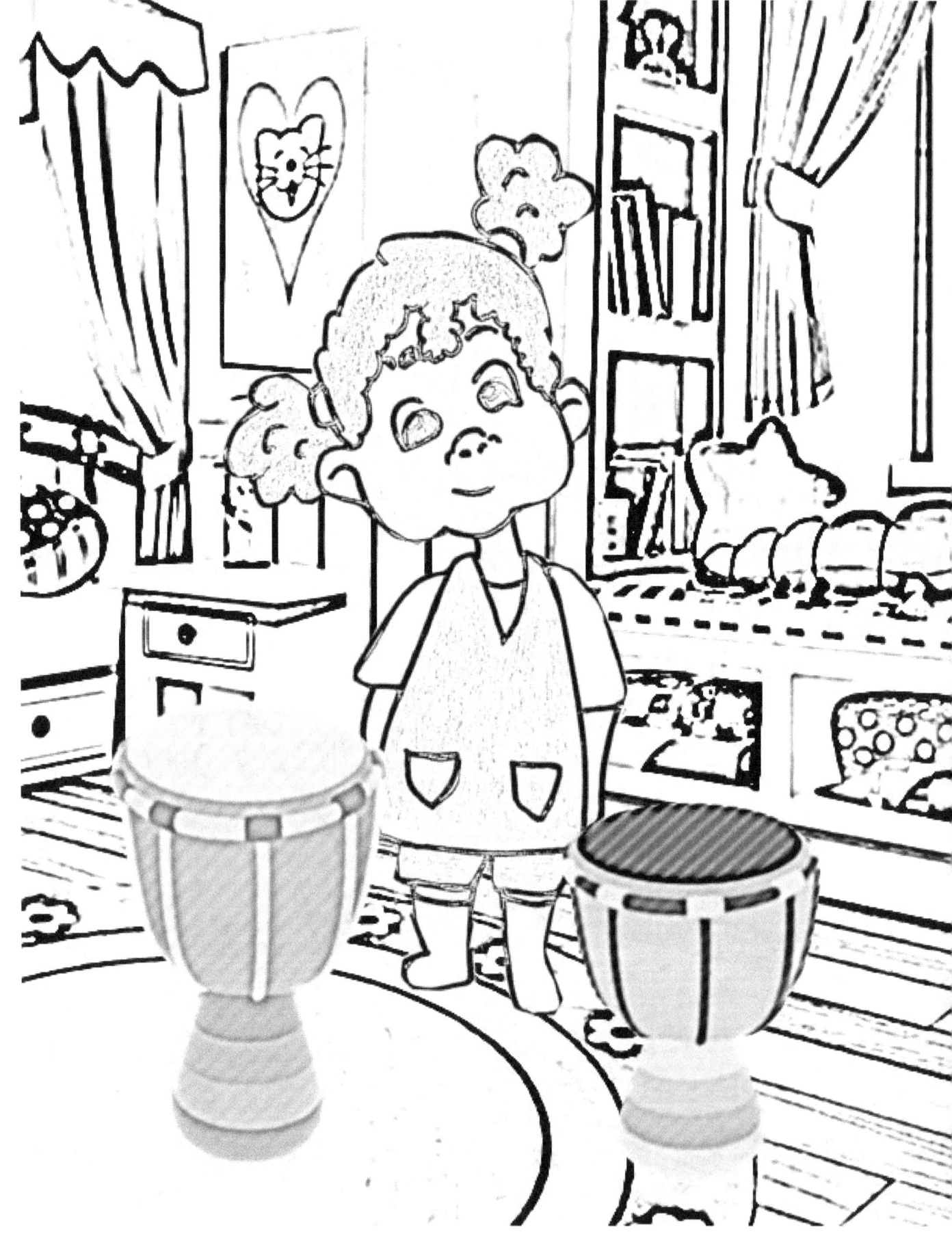

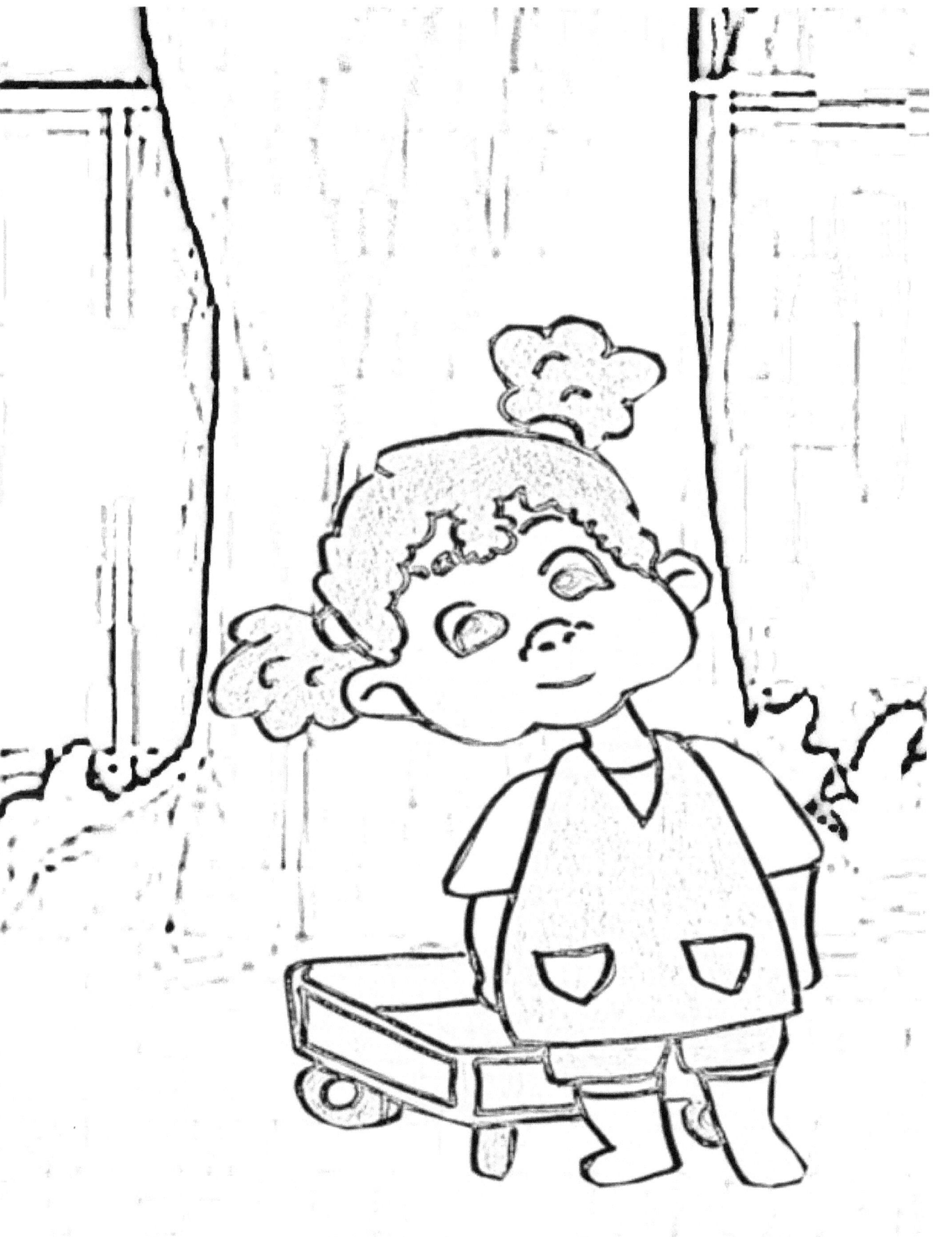

FREESTYLE DRAWING PAGES

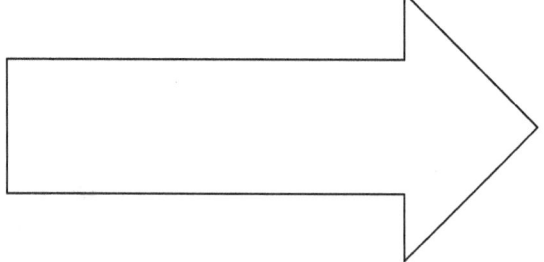

www.ingramcontent.com/pod-product-compliance
Lightning Source LLC
Chambersburg PA
CBHW062237220526
45471CB00009B/3517